How to Succeed as an Inventor / Showing the Wonderful Possibilities in the Field of Invention; c.

Goodwin B. Smith

PREFACE

The author of this book, after a number of years' experience in Patent Causes, is constrained to enter a strong protest against the enormous waste and loss attendant on methods at present pursued in regard to patents. This loss and waste is largely due to a lack of business knowledge necessary to properly market and develop inventions. History shows that enormous profits can be earned from good, strong patents.

A careful perusal of the following pages will point out some of the dangers to be avoided and the safe and reasonable course to be pursued. Invention is a matter that requires the deepest study, and should be approached, not in a haphazard, hit-or-miss fashion, but rather in a receptive, studious, analytical manner. While the average individual is fond of giving advice, no one enjoys accepting it. There is no one, however, who so needs competent, unprejudiced advice as the inventor.

A genius is more or less prejudiced in certain directions, and it has been found that the prejudice oftentimes runs against the acceptance of well-intentioned criticism.

"Our judgment is like our watches,—none go just alike, but each believes his own."

It is to be hoped that this volume will be the means of saving, as well as earning, money for the hosts of deserving American geniuses.

The Author.

Philadelphia, March, 1909.

CHAPTER I.

LOOKING FORWARD

"Patience and the investment of time and labor for future results are essential factors in every inventor's success."

The field of invention is closed to no one. The studious mechanic may design and improve on the machine he operates. The day laborer, if dissatisfied with his lot, may devise means for lessening the toil of his class, and largely increase his earning capacity. The busy housewife, not content with the drudgery incident to her household cares, may devise a means or article which will lighten her task, and prove a blessing to her sisters. The plodding clerk, without an iota of mechanical knowledge, may perfect a system or an office appliance which will prove of vast benefit to himself and his fellows. The scientist may discover new forces and make new applications of old principles which will make the world marvel,—and so on through the whole category of crafts, occupations and professions.

If one of the old Kings of Israel, centuries ago, voiced the sentiment that there was nothing new under the sun, do we not possess, at the present time, a similar mental attitude, and are we not apt to say with him that there appears to be "nothing new under the sun"? Civilization begets new needs and wants; opportunities for new invention are multiplying at a tremendous rate. In other words, where an inventor, two centuries ago, would have had one hundred chances to "make good," today the chances are multiplied many thousand-fold.

No avenue of business can open up the possibilities of such enormous honors and fabulous money returns as a *real* invention which is in universal demand. The discoveries of the past form a record which is not only glorious, but points the man of genius of today in an unswerving manner to the possibilities which the future holds, and which are vastly greater than anything which has gone before. Each age finds the people convinced that human ingenuity has reached the summit of achievement, but the future will find forces, mechanical principles and combinations which will excite wonder, and prove to be of incalculable benefit to mankind.

Our old friend Darius Green and his flying machine, that we heard about when we were children, was not as great a fool as he was imputed to be.

Witness at the present time the marvelous results attained by inventors with air ships. We are proud of Wilbur and Orville Wright, who at this writing have just broken all records for Aeroplanes, or "machines heavier than air." It seems that in five or ten years from now the navigation of the air will be a problem perfectly solved.

(Since writing the above, on Thursday, September 17th, Orville Wright, at Fort Myer, Va., met with an accident to his machine, which resulted in the death of Lieutenant Selfridge, of the U.S. Army, and severe injuries to the inventor. The accident is said to have been due to the breaking of one of the propellers.)

When you think that the first locomotives that were invented were considered wonders if they made a speed of eight to ten miles per hour, the chances are that within the next few years we will have airships going through space at incredible rates of speed.

We might also, at this time, refer to the experiments of Count Zeppelin and Santos-Dumont, and the American, Professor Baldwin, in "dirigible balloons." This type of airships will undoubtedly be superseded by the "Aeroplane," or the "Helicopter." The principal inventors in this line are Henry Farman, the French inventor, and Delagrange, the German. Wright Brothers hold the world's record, at this time.

Little did Murdock (who erected, in 1792, while an engineer in Cornwall, England, a little gasometer which produced gas enough to light his house and office) think that in the year 1908 no house would be considered as modern unless it was fully equipped with the gas for lighting and heating which he discovered and brought to practical use. It is also said that "while Murdock resided in Cornwall he made gas from every substance he could think of, and had bladders filled with it, with which, and his little steam carriage running on the road, he used to astonish the people." No one is astonished at "little steam carriages," or, in other words, automobiles, nowadays, one hundred and sixteen years later.

Our grandparents, when they were young people, imagined that they were living in the "Golden Age," and yet we today would consider their lack

6

of what we nowadays consider positive necessities a mighty primitive and inconvenient manner in which to live. When the "wisest man," centuries ago, is chronicled as saying, "There is nothing new under the sun," they lived in tents, rode camels, fought with bows and arrows, sling shots and battering rams! While the Tower of Babel was possibly the first "skyscraper," it did not contain express elevators, hot and cold water, telephones, call boxes, yale locks, granolithic floors, fire escapes, transom lifts, automatic sprinklers, stationary wash stands, water closets, steam or hot water heat, electric and gas lights, push buttons, sash weights, and so on ad infinitum. So you can readily appreciate the marvelous strides the human race is making in the way of material development, and all, or nearly all of which has been due to the fertile brain and nimble wit of the inventors! Who will have the temerity to say when and where this development will stop, when Solomon, centuries ago, thought they had reached the limit?

What will be the next wonderful invention? For instance, the perfected telephote? You, by stepping into a cabinet in Philadelphia, could have your photograph taken and shown in Boston, all by and through an electric wire! The Telephote may transmit light and color as the Telephone does sound; why not a combination of the two, so you can see your friend perfectly when you talk to him on the 'phone?

Our grandparents thought they were as comfortable as possible, and they were, because they did not know any better. Do we know better? One hundred years from now, possibly, *our* great, great-grandchildren will consider us as having lived in the "stone age." The field of invention has no bars up,—you, all of us, are free to enter.

"The important thing in life is to have a great aim, and to possess the aptitude and perseverance to attain it."

CHAPTER II.

LOOKING BACKWARD

"Intelligent study and the application of unremitting effort to a definite purpose are the factors that overcome obstacles."

Here follows a list of the principal inventions chronologically arranged, with the names and nationalities of their inventors.

Year. Name of Invention. Name of Inventor. Nationality. 1620 Spirally grooved rifle barrel Blaew German. 1643 Barometer Torricelli Italian. 1660 Discovery of Electrical Phenomena William Gilbert English. 1663 Steam engine Thos. Newcomen English. 1690 Steam engine with piston Denis Papin French. 1702 First practical application of steam engine Thos. Savory English. 1709 Thermometer Fahrenheit Danzig. 1725 Franklin printing press Benj. Franklin U.S. 1731 Stereotyping William Ged Scotch. 1733 Weaving flying shuttle John Kay English. 1745 Leyden Jar Kleist German. 1752 Lightning conductor Benj. Franklin U.S. 1763 Spinning jenny Jos. Hargreaves English. 1767 Piano England. 1775 Cut nails Jere. Wilkinson U.S. 1777 Circular wood saw Miller English. 1782 Steam engine Jas. Watt Scotch. 1783 Balloon inflated with gas Montgolfier French. 1784 Puddling iron Henry Cort English. 1784 Cast iron plow Jas. Small Scotch. 1786 Steamboat John Fitch U.S. 1787 Steam road wagon, first automobile Oliver Evans U.S. 1788 Threshing machine And. Meikle English. 1791 Wood planer Sam'l Bentham English. 1794 Cotton gin Eli Whitney U.S. 1800 Electric battery Volta Italian. 1801 Fire-proof safe Richard Scott English. 1803 Steel pen Wise English. 1804 Malleable iron castings Lucas English. 1808 Band wood saw Newberry English. 1808 First sea-going steamboat John Stephens U.S. 1810 Revolving cylinder printing press Fred'k Koenig German. 1811 Breech-loading shot gun Thornton & Hall U.S. 1814 First locomotive, U.S Geo. Stephenson English. 1815 Miner safety lamp Sir Humphry Davy English. 1815 Gas meter Clegg English. 1823 Discovery of water gas Ibbetson English. 1825 Portland cement Aspdim English. 1827 Friction matches John Walker U.S. 1828 Hot blast for iron furnaces Neilson Scotch. 1829 Washington printing press Sam'l Rust U.S. 1831 Chloroform Guthrie Scotch. 1832 Electric telegraph Prof.

Morse U.S. 1832 Rotary electric motor Sturgeon English. 1832 "Old Iron Sides" locomotive Baldwin U.S. 1833 Steam whistle Geo. Stephenson English. 1834 Reaper Cyrus H. McCormick U.S. 1834 Carbolic acid Runge German. 1835 Horse-shoe machine Burden U.S. 1836 Acetylene gas Davy English. 1836 Revolver Sam'l Colt U.S. 1836 Screw propeller for steam navigation John Erickson U.S. 1837 Galvanizing iron Craufurd English. 1839 Babbitt metal Isaac Babbit U.S. 1839 Vulcanizing rubber Goodyear U.S. 1839 Daguerreotype Louis Daguerre French. 1840 Artesian wells   French. 1842 Automatic piano Seytre French. 1844 First telegram sent Prof. Morse U.S. 1845 Double cylinder printing press Richard Hoe U.S. 1845 Pneumatic tire Thompson English. 1846 Sewing machine Elias Howe U.S. 1846 Ether as an anaesthetic Dr. Morton U.S. 1847 Nitroglycerine Sobrero   1847 Improved Hoe printing press Richard Hoe U.S. 1849 Steam pressure gauge Bourdon French. 1849 Corliss engine George H. Corliss U.S. 1850 Mercerized cotton John Mercer English. 1851 Breech-loading rifle Maynard U.S. 1851 Ice-making machine Gorrie U.S. 1852 Telegraph fire alarm Channing & Farmer U.S. 1854 Diamond rock drill Herman U.S. 1854 Revolver Smith & Wesson U.S. 1855 Cocaine Gaedeke German. 1855 Bessemer steel Sir Henry Bessemer English. 1855 Bicycle Michaux French. 1856 Sleeping car Woodruff U.S. 1858 Cable car Gardner U.S. 1858 First Atlantic cable Cyrus Field U.S. 1859 "Great Eastern" launched   U.S. 1861 Passenger elevator E. G. Otis U.S. 1861 Barbed wire fence   U.S. 1862 Gattling gun Dr. R. J. Gattling U.S. 1865 Antiseptic surgery Sir Jos. Lister English. 1866 Open hearth steel process Siemens-Martin English. 1866 Torpedoes Whitehead U.S. 1868 Typewriting machine C. L. Sholes U.S. 1868 Dynamite Nobel French. 1868 Oleomargarine Mege French. 1868 Sulky plow Slusser U.S. 1869 Spring tooth harrow Garver U.S. 1870 Celluloid Hyatt U.S. 1872 Automatic brake Geo. Westinghouse U.S. 1872 Car coupler E. H. Janney U.S. 1873 Quadruplex telegraph Thos. A. Edison U.S. 1873 Twine binder harvester Gorham U.S. 1873 Self-binding reaper Loche & Wood U.S. 1875 Roller flour mills Wegmann U.S. 1875 Ice-making machine Pictet Switzerland. 1876 Telephone Dr. Alex. Graham Bell U.S. 1877 Phonograph Thos. A. Edison U.S. 1877 Gas engine N. A. Otto U.S. 1877 Telephone transmitter Emile Berliner U.S. 1878 Carbon filament for electric lamps Thos. A. Edison U.S. 1878 Rotary disc cultivator Mallon U.S. 1880

Telephone transmitter Blake U.S. 1880 Hammerless gun Greener U.S. 1880 Typhoid bacillus Robert Koch German. 1880 Pneumonia bacillus Sternberg U.S. 1881 Buttonhole machine Reece U.S. 1882 Tuberculosis bacillus Robert Koch German. 1882 Hydrophobia bacillus Louis Pasteur French. 1884 Cholera bacillus Robert Koch German. 1884 Diphtheria bacillus Loefler German. 1884 Lockjaw bacillus Nicolaier French. 1884 Antipyrene Kuno U.S. 1884 Linotype machine Ottmar Mergenthaler U.S. 1885 First electric street railway in the U.S. Baltimore, Md. 1885 Overhead electric trolley Van Depole U.S. 1886 Graphophone Bell & Tainter U.S. 1887 Cyanide process McArthur & Forest U.S. 1887 Incandescent gas light Carl Welsbach German. 1888 Harveyized armor plate Harvey U.S. 1888 Kodak snapshot camera Eastman & Walker U.S. 1890 Bicycles equipped with pneumatic tires U.S. 1890 Magazine rifle Krag-Jorgensen U.S. 1891 Rotary steam turbine Parsons English. 1893 Kinetoscope Thos. A. Edison U.S. 1893 Carborundum E. G. Acheson U.S. 1893 Calcium carbide electrically produced Thos. L. Wilson U.S. 1895 Liquifying air Carl Linde German. 1895 X-rays Prof. Roentgen German. 1895 Acetylene gas from calcium carbide Thos. L. Wilson U.S. 1896 Wireless telegraphy G. Marconi Italian. 1896 Finsen rays Finsen Danish. 1898 Non-whittling lead pencil F. H. Lippincott U.S. 1900 Mercury vapor electric light Peter Cooper Hewitt U.S. 1901 Airship M. Santos-Dumont French. 1901 Automobile mower Deering Harvester Co. U.S. From the Encyclopedia Americana.

"There are no elevators in the house of success."—Silent Partner.

Since the above list (taken from the Encyclopedia Americana) was published, there have been a large number of very important inventions brought out.

In 1898 Professor and Madam Curie, of Paris, discovered radium. This remarkable substance is extracted from pitch-blende. It is said to require the reduction of about five thousand tons of the blende to produce one pound of radium. The cost of one pound of radium is variously estimated at from one to three millions of dollars. Radium overturns all the laws of chemistry and physics. Scientists state that if a method of producing it cheaply is ever discovered it will create the greatest revolution in industrial circles. One pound of radium is said to be capable of lighting an enormous area for one billion years without reducing its size or substance by one

10

thousandth part. In other words, it exerts abnormal energy without any appreciable loss.

In 1902, January, Peter Cooper Hewitt, of New York City, announced the invention by him of his Mercury Vapor tube electric light. This light is red-less,—gives off all colors except red. It is in present use in many large establishments. It is practically indestructible, and gives eight times as much light with the same amount of electricity as other lights. Mr. Hewitt is a wealthy man, having inherited money. He comes of the famous New York Hewitt family, whose members have been in the forefront of progress. Mr. Hewitt also invented the "Hewitt Electrical Converter" and the "Hewitt Electrical Interrupter," both inventions of unusual merit.

In 1903, January 18th, Guglielmo Marconi sent a wireless message from Cape Cod, Mass., to Cornwall, England, a distance of 3000 miles. Such a thing, a few years ago, would have been considered absolutely impossible,—unbelievable,—a wild flight of the imagination. Marconi's achievement was accomplished only after the most prolonged experimentation and many disappointments.

In 1908, September 12th, Hudson Maxim filed an application for a patent on an electrical invention for the prolongation of human life.

In 1908, Professor Alexander Graham Bell and Professor Emile Berliner, famous inventors in telephones, are working on new styles of flying machines. With these experts in the field, aerial navigation will, no doubt, shortly be a problem completely solved.

NOTES.

In 200 B.C., Hero, of Alexandria, gives an account of an ingenious steam toy.

In 1543, one Blasco de Garay is said to have shown in the harbor of Barcelona, Spain, a vessel of two hundred tons' burden, moved by a paddle wheel driven by steam power.

In 1663 Edward Somerset, the ingenious Marquis of Worcester, contrived the first steam engine.

In 1742, when Benjamin Franklin invented the "Franklin Stove," or as it is sometimes called, the "Pennsylvania Fireplace," he refused to accept a patent on it, saying, "we enjoy great advantages from the inventions of

11

others, so we should be glad of an opportunity to serve others by an invention of ours." An unscrupulous London manufacturer made some light changes in Franklin's stove, we are sorry to state, got a patent on it, and made a fortune from its sale.

An invention of the greatest utility was that brought out in 1788 by William Symington, a young Englishman, for a method of converting the reciprocating motion of an engine into the rotary.

About 1790, Claude Chappe, a Frenchman, while at school at Angers, contrived an apparatus consisting of a post bearing a revolving beam and circulatory arms with which he conveyed signals to three of his brothers who were at another school about half-a-league distant, who read the signals with a telescope. In 1792 the French Legislature voted Chappe 6000 francs ($1200) to enable him to make experiments in Paris. This invention of Chappe was called the "Semaphore Telegraph." Of course, misty or foggy weather would preclude the use of this signalling device. During the war between England and France an amusing incident is related of the use of the "Semaphore Telegraph." The admiral at Plymouth started a "wigwag message" to Whitehall, but was able to forward only part of the message, a thick fog gathering over a portion of the line and interrupting the message. The first part of the message was "Wellington defeated," which caused great distress and anxiety in London. The remainder of the message, "the French at Salamanca," received next day, changed the metropolitan sorrow into gladness.

About the year 1790, Signor Galvani, a professor of anatomy at Bologna, discovered the principle of Galvanic electricity. This was brought about in a very peculiar way. Mrs. Galvani was ill, and her physician prescribed some frog broth. Accordingly, frogs were procured, skinned, washed and laid on a table in the professor's laboratory, which seemed to serve a double purpose of a room for scientific and culinary operations. One of the professor's assistants was engaged in experimenting with a large electric machine which stood upon the same table, and had occasion to draw sparks from the machine. The wife of Galvani, who was present, was surprised to observe that every time he did so the limbs of the frogs moved as if alive. She immediately communicated this strange incident to her husband, who repeated the experiments with, of course, the same result.

From this experiment was later developed the so-called zinc and copper wet jars used in the art.

In 1807, Robert Fulton, who was of Irish Descent, made his famous trip in his steamboat, the "Clermont," from New York to Albany, a distance of one hundred and fifty miles, in thirty-two hours, and returned in thirty hours, averaging about five miles per hour. Many stories are told of the consternation the "Clermont" excited in those who saw her for the first time. People who had seen her passing at night described her as "a monster moving on the waters, defying wind and tide, and breathing flames and smoke." The steamboats, at that time, used pine wood for fuel, which sent columns of ignited vapor many feet above the stack, and whenever the fire was stirred enormous showers of sparks would fly off, which in the night produced a very brilliant and beautiful effect. Sailors and seamen on vessels that had never seen a steamboat were scared speechless, and in many cases prostrated themselves, and besought Providence to protect them from the approaches of the horrible monster which they saw.

In 1835 Thomas D. Edmundson, a station agent on the New Castle and Carlisle line, in England, invented the first railroad ticket. The inventor for several years devoted himself entirely to the ticket industry, and by degrees a business arose which became one of the largest in the world.

In 1840 the Government issued the first postage stamps.

George Stephenson died in 1848 at the age of 67, a wealthy man, beloved and honored by all. Statues of him were erected at Liverpool, London and Newcastle. In Rome, Italy, a tablet bears this inscription: "In this Rome, from whence wondrous roads proceed to the empire of the world, the employees of the Roman railways, on the 9th of June, 1881, worthily commemorated the centenary of George Stephenson, who opened still more wondrous roads to the brotherhood of the nations, and whose virtues, inspiring to great works, have left an undying example." During an examination before a Parliamentary Committee George Stephenson was asked, "Suppose, now, one of your engines to be going at the rate of nine or ten miles an hour, and that a cow were to stray upon the line, and get in the way of the engine, would not that be a very awkward circumstance?" Stephenson replied, "Yes, very awkward for the cow." In the course of the same examination he was asked, "But would not men and animals become

13

frightened by the red hot smoke pipe?" to which question Stephenson replied, "But how would they know that it was not painted?" These extracts indicate some of the difficulties inventors had to contend with.

In 1876 two hours after Bell filed his patent for his telephone, Elisha Gray, of Boston, filed an application for a similar device. Bell won, and has been awarded great honors for his invention. It was at first referred to as a "scientific toy." It is now a necessity.

In 1880 Marthelemay Themonier, a Frenchman, was mobbed for building a sewing machine, by laborers who thought his machines contrary to their interests.

"Victory belongs to the most persevering."—Napoleon.

"Success is the child of audacity."—Beaconsfield.

By-Products

Many men mistake obstinacy for perseverance.

Anybody can slide down hill, but it takes good legs and good wind to go up.

A third of our lives is spent in bed—that's why we ought to hustle the other two-thirds.

Waste is criminal. The old proverb says, "Waste not, want not." And it is true.

Anybody may drink at the fountain of knowledge, but you've got to bring your own cup.

The farther you look back into the history of industry and invention, the more you will be impressed with the fact that almost everything has improved as our ability to produce it has increased.

Wireless telegraphy would never have come about had not the other kind preceded, and it is impossible to imagine the phonograph's being ahead of the telephone.

Without illuminating gas and gasoline, Welsbach lights would never have been thought of or possible.

We would have no electric lights without the dynamo, and no dynamo if wire-drawing had not first been perfected.

So it goes—everything is dependent on factors that have preceded and any achievement of today is the result of thousands of years of previous effort and thought.

And the knowledge that we are adding to the world's store today is but the foundation for further advance by men to come.

As long as we don't know everything there will be things we cannot explain and these things will be called chance. Into the life of every human being there enter these inexplicable occurrences.

Silent Partner.

CHAPTER III.

PATENTS THE GREATEST SOURCE OF WEALTH

"Upon what meat does this, our Caesar, feed, that he has grown so great?"—Shakespeare.
THE SOURCES OF WEALTH.

The diagram below shows very clearly the rich men of the world, and the source of their wealth. The cry nowadays is that there are no chances for accumulating wealth as did these people—in some ways this is right.

Three of the avenues to wealth are pretty well closed. Taking each up in turn we find 1st. Natural Wealth.

Secured by Mining, Drilling and Digging. Examples:
John D. Rockefeller,
Henry H. Rogers,
Barney Barnato,
and many others.

First.

Mines and Oil Wells are becoming scarcer every year, and there are few which remain undiscovered. 2nd. Real Estate.

Advances in value as by buying lots in a growing city and taking advantage of its growth. Examples:
Hetty Green,
The Vanderbilts,
Russell Sage,
and many others.

Second.

Real Estate takes an inside knowledge of conditions, which none but men who give the subject deep study can hope to acquire.   3rd. Transportation.

Steam Railways, Electric Railways, and Steamboat lines. Examples:
The Goulds,
Thomas J. Ryan,
E. H. Harriman.

Third.

Transportation requires big capital, and the small investor on the "outside" has no chance whatsoever.   4th. Patents.

Inventions on articles in use in the manufactures, the arts, the home. Examples:
Carnegie,
Edison,
Schwab,
Maxim,
Krupp,
Westinghouse,
Pullman,
Bell,
Welsbach,
Singer,
Hewitt,
McCormick,
Acheson,
Colt,
Marconi,
Bessemer,
and thousands of others.

Fourth.

PATENTS ARE TO-DAY THE GREATEST SOURCE OF WEALTH.

"Genius, that power which dazzles mortal eyes, Is oft but perseverance in disguise."

CHAPTER IV.

SUCCESSFUL INVENTORS

"Lives of great men all remind us, We can make our lives sublime, And departing, leave behind us, Footprints on the sands of time."—Longfellow.

The long list of famous patentees with their inventions which a previous chapter contains is an eloquent testimonial to the fact that fame, fortune and an undying place in history will be given to anyone fortunate enough to conceive and work out a new idea which inures to the benefit of mankind. While these famous inventors have been devising and exploiting inventions of wide scope and large calibre there have been an army of small inventors which should be equally as famous and whose inventions will, probably, on the average, return larger proportionate profits to their owners than have a great many of the prominent ones already listed. The writer has in mind small inventions, such as, for instance, Mrs. Pott's Sad Iron; the De Long Hook and Eye; the Gillette Safety Razor; Enterprise Meat Chopper; Junoform Bust Form; Push-point Pencil; Bromo Seltzer; Morrow Coaster Brake; Brass Tips for Boys' Shoes; Mennen's Talcum Powder; Rubber Tips for Lead Pencils; Bundy Time Clock; President Suspenders; Pianola; Castoria; Angelus; O'Sullivan's Rubber Heel; Macey's Sectional Bookcases; Red Dwarf Ink Pencil; 1900 Washing Machine; Tyden Table Lock, and the thousands of similar small inventions, practically all of which are bringing or have brought enormous fortunes to their owners and developers.

King C. Gillette has become a wealthy man from the royalties and profits on his safety razor. While safety razors had been on the market for years, it took Gillette to bring out a better one, patent it, and make his fortune. The inventor of the President Suspender is said to have collected over fifty thousand dollars last year in royalties on the sales of over two hundred thousand dozen pairs of his suspenders. Miss Wolfe, the inventor of the Junoform Bust Form, it was remarked recently, would attain wealth from her royalties. Mrs. Potts is reputed to have collected over half a million dollars from royalties from the patents on her sad iron.

It is also said that the Selden Gas Engine royalties exceed ten million dollars in amount. It is stated that McCormick, the inventor of a Cream Separator, has an annual income from his patents of over thirty thousand dollars. It is said that the inventor of the new-style "pay-as-you-enter" street car will receive a large royalty on every car of that style used in the United

States. They are at present coming into use on the metropolitan street car lines. Everybody is familiar with the enormous fortune made by Pullman with his palace car patents.

NOTES.

It is related that when George Westinghouse called on Commodore Vanderbilt to endeavor to interest him in his air-brake, Vanderbilt said to him: "Do you mean to tell me that you can stop a train of cars by wind?" and when informed that in effect that was what was contemplated, remarked that he had no time for fools. Sometime afterward when, through the support of Andrew Carnegie and several others, a successful test of the brake had been made, Westinghouse had the satisfaction, according to the story, of replying to Vanderbilt's request for a conference, "I have no time to waste on fools."

Ottmar Mergenthaler worked twenty years on the development of his linotype machine, and ten years thereafter in perfecting it. The Mergenthaler Linotype Company has paid out twenty millions of dollars in dividends in fourteen years. The romance of the invention of the linotype brings out in glaring letters PERSISTENCE, as Edward Mott Woolley states in "System," of September, 1908, in an article describing the development of the linotype machine.

It is related of Oscar Hammerstein, the well-known theatrical proprietor, that when he was fifteen years old he landed from a steamer at the Battery in New York, after running away from his German home. He was without money or friends, or any place to go. He got a job in a cigar factory at $2.00 per week. Making cigars by hand seemed to him a poor way of doing it, so he began experimenting on his own account, and four years later he had a machine to do the work. He sold this machine for $6,000 cash, and immediately started on a new one, which in place of selling outright he had manufactured on a royalty basis. It is said that he has received over $250,000 in cash from his royalties. Yet today Hammerstein is not known by his inventions, but by the big theatrical enterprises which have earned or lost other fortunes for him at various times.

In the struggle of Charles Goodyear to manufacture a rubber compound that should fulfil mercantile needs is presented a striking, if rather familiar example of what eternal persistence will finally accomplish, and of how it may be assisted by what we call "luck." When he was twenty-one Goodyear entered a rubber house in Philadelphia and began experimenting in India rubber. By chance one day a little rubber mixed with sulphur fell on a stove, and he at once realized what might be accomplished by what is now known as vulcanization. To carry on his experiments he was required to pawn the school-books of his children to raise money. However, he kept everlastingly at it, and was rewarded with a number of international prizes and decorated by several foreign rulers. His name has gone down to fame as one of the successful inventors of the world. The Goodyear Rubber Company bears his name.

The public today is familiar with the record of Thomas A. Edison, who is considered the greatest inventor the world has ever known. The new book which has recently come out, "The Life of Thomas A. Edison," is well worth purchasing and reading. The public press reported he had won his infringement suits and that the "Moving Picture" trust or combination agreed to pay him royalties running into a sum of seven figures.

George Ade, the "funny man," is independent financially from the royalties paid him on his copyrights.

The story of the De Long Hook and Eye Company is the history of an infinitesimal start with an enormous present size.

Sir Henry Bessemer is said to have been paid $10,000,000 in royalties on his steel process.

Emerson, a Baltimore druggist, made a number of fortunes from his invention of Bromo-Seltzer. Likewise Mennen, of talcum powder fame, whose face and name are known all over the world.

Landis, a Franklin county (Pa.) man, sold his "Straw Stacker" patents, it is said, for $50,000 cash,—practically all profit.

This list, if complete, would fill volumes, but it would be a story with the same ending in each and every case.

A careful study of the reason why all the above patents have proved to be so successful emphasizes the fact that inventors, to succeed, *must not lose sight of the Six Cardinal Tests enumerated elsewhere in this volume.*

REMIND US OF INVENTIONS THAT HAVE BROUGHT FAME AND WEALTH   REMIND US OF INVENTIONS THAT HAVE BROUGHT FAME AND WEALTH

CHAPTER V.

FIELD OF INVENTION

"If a man can write a better book, preach a better sermon, or make a better mouse-trap than his neighbor, though he build his house in the woods, the world will make a beaten pathway to his door."—Emerson.

Inventions, to possess commercial merit, must supersede in utility similar devices already on the market. They must also possess capacity for production at lower cost, as well as having conspicuously superior merit. The field of invention is a broad one, and embraces any new electrical appliances, engineering devices, improvements in steam navigation, agricultural implements, railways, household novelties, novelties in hardware and tools, pencils and toys, vehicles, furniture, toilet articles, wearing apparel, office appliances and devices.

INVENTIONS AND IMPROVEMENTS NEEDED.

Electrical.

A simple, cheap and powerful electric motor; electrical motors adapted to use of either direct or alternating current; improvements in the filaments of incandescent bulbs, something along the lines of the new Tungsten filaments; new, cheap substitute for gutta-percha for insulating; simple method of generating ozone for medical and disinfecting purposes; method for generating electricity direct from coal without the incidental production of light and heat; a new, indestructible incandescent lamp filament; a new style of incandescent lamp that will give more light and use less current; a simple means for preventing the blowing out of fuses, and yet preventing the overloading of the motors; method of extracting electricity from the earth. (NOTE: A number of experiments have been carried out along this line with partial success.) A method of storing electricity generated during a severe electrical storm. (NOTE: This is not considered practicable by electrical engineers, although it is possible that someone may hit on a way

of accomplishing it.) A simple, light accumulator for storing electricity.
Chemical.

A substitute for paper pulp; strong, tough, thin, flexible paper; substitute for glass in eye-glasses, telescopes, opera glasses, and other optical lenses; a cheap, artificial substitute for indigo; method for deodorizing petroleum, gasoline, naphtha and similar volatile oils without changing their quality; method of deodorizing asphalt; method of deodorizing paint; method of increasing the life and durableness of soft rubber; simple means for preserving butter; new shoe blacking free from sulphuric and acetic acids; cheap substitute for matches; method of removing nicotine from tobacco; method of utilizing vulcanized rubber scrap; substitute for leather; method for producing artificial mica in large sheets; artificial flavors of tea and coffee, similar to the commercial artificial extract of vanilla; cheap method of producing sugar from starch; method of producing pure carbon; substitute for celluloid; substitute for asphalt; method for producing flexible glass.

Mining and Metallurgy.

First and foremost is the method of hardening and tempering copper; cheap method for extracting gold from brick clay, ore, sand, etc.; cheap method for procuring iron direct from ore without the intervention of the blast furnace; method for producing malleable pig iron; cheap method of producing high-speed steels for tools and the like; machine to separate slate from Anthracite and Bituminous Coal. (NOTE: It should be some process not requiring water settling-tanks.) Process for casting copper without blow holes; solder for cast iron; cheap method for recovering tin from old tin cans and the like.

Railways and Military.

Note.—It has been found extremely hard to introduce railway patents. We would, therefore, most earnestly advise our American inventors not to spend any time and money on inventions such as car couplers, steel railway ties, block signals, and the like. In this class we would suggest so-called "small-inventions."

Efficient air gun as a weapon; improvements in army tents;

improvements in dirigible balloons and aeroplanes for military uses.* (*NOTE: This is a big undertaking, and we would not advise any of our clients to enter it.)

Machinery, Tools, Steam Engines, Etc.

Simple means of adjusting ball bearings; attachment for lathes, such as taper cutting devices, grinding attachments; attachments for planers for producing curved surfaces; attachment for drill press for radial boring; new and improved tools of all kinds and descriptions; simple and cheap bone crusher; simple and cheap bone cleaner; simple and cheap casting machine for small foundries; simple and cheap molding machine for small foundries; machine for casting under pressure; substitute for fly wheels on engines; efficient safety stopping devices for engines; substitute for governor; cheap and efficient denatured alcohol motor; substitute for belts and pulleys; simple, cheap and efficient anti-friction bearings; machine for automatically sewing buttons on clothing; tool for cutting ice without waste; cheap music turner.

Recording and Vending Machines, Office Appliances, Etc.

Simple, cheap and efficient cash register; cash register that will throw out false coins; machine for vending newspapers; electrically driven typewriter; cheap substitute for fountain pen; cheap substitute for lead pencil; indestructible writing pen; reliable gas meter; reservoir lettering brush.

Lighting, Heating and Ventilating—Building Construction.

Indestructible gas mantel for Welsbach lights; method of simultaneously lighting all the burners in a room, or house; automatic valve closing device for shutting off gas when not ignited; brick-laying machine; method of glazing without the use of putty; window sash that will not bind or stick in the frame; substitute for sash weights; substitute for spring shade rollers; substitute for carpet nails; new, cheap, springless lock; substitute for hinges on doors; cheap, efficient door check and buffer.

Auto Vehicles.

Durable and unpuncturable tires; cheap and efficient power meter;

cheap and efficient dust preventer; improvements in all the details of automobile and vehicular construction; substitute for motor wheels.

Miscellaneous.

Textile:

Substitute for horse hair; substitute for broom fibre; substitute for asbestos; substitute for silk; method of coating cheap fibres with silk; method of spinning asbestos; substitute for an umbrella; one-piece covering for umbrellas, etc., etc.

Printing:

Method for multi-color printing with but one impression; method for printing sheet metals; substitute for printing blocks.* (*NOTE: Must be light in weight, and non-inflammable.) Substitute for lithographic stone; a firm, black, copying, printing ink; method for photographing in colors.

Agricultural.

Machine for harvesting sugar cane; substitute for cotton bale tie; method or machine for exterminating caterpillars; method or machine for exterminating mosquitoes; improvements or new devices for use of farmers, agriculturalists, truckmen, florists, and similar vocations; method or machine for annihilating flies.

General.

Substitute for rubber fire hose; method for profitable utilization of saw dust; substitute for hair pin, or one that will not fall out; envelope that cannot be opened.

WHAT NOT TO INVENT.

Non-refillable bottles.

Nut locks.

Metal railway ties.

Railroad rail joints.

Patent medicines.

Car couplers.

Hooks and eyes.

Safety pins.

Hair curlers.

Washing Compounds.

Trolley pole catchers.

Bending machines, unless absolutely new idea, and style.

Adding machines, unless absolutely new idea and style.

Present style typewriters.

Turbine engines, unless absolutely new idea, and style.

Submarine boats.

Our reason for advising inventors to stay away from the above classes is on account of the fact of the killing competition in these classes, and the additional fact that the field is absolutely overcrowded. The attorneys that have applied for the hosts of patents for inventors in these lines have "rung all possible changes" in their claims for patents into which it is possible to twist and turn the English language.

Wants Fulfilled.

In a publication on Patents published about fifteen years ago, the following articles were asked for, which have since been invented, and which are making their inventors money:

Cheap ice machine.

Denaturated alcohol.

Cheap calcium carbide.

Method of preserving milk.

(Note the organization of the "White Cross Milk Companies" in the cities of Philadelphia, Boston, New York, Baltimore and Washington, at this writing. Milk prepared by this process is said to keep for several months, and will be absolutely free from germs and bacilli. It is a new process.)

Smokeless gun powder (now in almost general use).

Iron and steel railway ties. (They have been found mechanically impracticable and have been discarded by the Pennsylvania Railroad Company.)

Safety device for rifles and revolvers. (Everybody is familiar with the "Hammer the Hammer" advertisement.)

Milking machine.

Bread cutting machine.

Pocket cigar lighter.

Steam heating for trains.

The above list will serve as an illustration of the fact that inventors are persistently supplying what the world needs in the way of new devices and machines.

SUPPLY AND DEMAND.

"Where there's a will there's a way."

Do not imagine that anyone is lying awake at night waiting for your invention to come out, because they are not. All of us consider ourselves pretty comfortable, and we are not bothering much about any new inventions. Another mistake inventors often make is that of endeavoring to make the public want their device. The proper thing to do is to invent something that the public already wants. In other words, "follow the lines of least resistance."

There are many good things which are very ingenious, and perfectly novel and patentable, but which are in lines in which there would not be enough sale in ten years to pay the inventor the expense of getting out patents. Yet plenty of such things are patented almost every week, in this country. "Some time there could be but one customer,—say, the government, or some great corporation,—and there may be reasons which are obvious, and others not so plain on the surface, why you could not even make them a present of your invention."

CHAPTER VI.

GROWTH OF THE FIELD OF INVENTION

The following pages concisely show the marvelous growth of the Field of Invention from Primitive Man's Three Fundamental Wants, namely, Food, Clothing and Shelter, to the present-day countless necessities of Twentieth Century life. The same marvelous broadening of the field is found in all directions. The few illustrations given on the following pages will illustrate the point, and direct the thoughts of the student unerringly to the almost illimitable sphere of invention.

CHART PARTIALLY ILLUSTRATING THE VAST GROWTH OF THE
FIELD OF INVENTION FROM PRIMITIVE MAN'S THREE
FUNDAMENTAL NEEDS TO THE PRESENT DAY
ESSENTIALS OF CIVILIZATION.

chart
FOOD

H Scythes, **A** Sickles, **R** Rakes, Reapers, **PLANTING** { Garden Tools, Plows, Harrows, Rollers, Planters, Seed Drills, etc. **V** Mowers, **E** Binders, **S** Threshers, **T** Stackers, **CULTIVATING** { Cultivators, Sprinklers, Weeders, Insect Destroyers, Fertilizers, etc. **I** Loaders, **N** Unloaders, **G** Grain-elevators, etc.

STOCK RAISING { Fences, Harness, Incubators, Brooders, Milking Machines, Creameries, etc.

M Crates, Boxes, **A** Stores, Scales, **R** Packages, **SLAUGHTERING** { Conveyors, Pens, Grinders, Stuffers, etc. **K** Delivery-systems, **E** Office Appliances, **T** Stationery, **I** Printing, **HUNTING** { Bows and Arrows, Snares, Traps, Guns, Bags, etc. **N** Pens, Pencils, **G** Inks, Rubbers, etc.

P Cutlery, **R** Stoves, **E** Kettles, **FISHING** { Nets, Hooks, Lines, Boats, Canneries, Kits, etc. **P** Broilers, **A** Ovens, **R** Condiments, **I** Grinding, **N** Distilling, **G** Evaporating, etc.

S Elevators, **T** Refrigerators, **O** Canning, **R** Curing, **I** Drying, **N** Pickling, **G** Evaporating, etc.

A **M** Musical **U** Instruments, **S** Theatres, **E** Parks, **M** Cards, **E** Games, **N** Toys, **T** Moving **S** Pictures, etc. Copyright 1909, by Goodwin B. Smith.

SHELTER

C Tools, Engineering **F** Carpets, Rugs, **O** Excavating, **U** Fixtures, **N** Masonry, **R** Furniture, **S** Wood-working, **N** Bedding, **T** Elevating, **I** China, **R** Stone-cutting, **S** Cutlery, **U** etc. **H** Glass-ware, **C T I O N.** **I** Periodicals, **N** Books, **G** etc.

HARDWARE { Builders, Shelf, Mill House, etc. **D** Sling shots, Bows **E** Burglar Alarms, Armor, **F** Revolvers, Shot, **E** and Arrows, Guns, **N** Military Battle Ships, **D** Insurance: Fire, Life, **CLEANING** { Brooms, Brushes Sweepers, Soaps, etc. **I** Accident, Burglary, **N** Liability, etc. **G** Explosives, Air-ships, etc.

M Quarrying, **A** **T** Cement, **E** **R** Plaster, **I** **HEATING** { Brasiers, Stoves, Furnaces, Hot air, Hot water, Steam, Vapor, Electricity, etc. **A** Steel-Structure, **L** **S** etc.

DECORATING { Paint, Varnish, Wall Paper, Molding, Carving, Polishing, Photography, etc.

MEDICINE { Drugs, Instruments, Specifics, Toxins, etc.

LIGHTING { Lamps, Burners, Oil, Gas, Electricity, Acetylene, Glass, etc.

31

CLOTHING

M Spinning, Weaving, **A** Bleaching, Tanning, **N** Curing, Sorting, Picking, **U** Carding, Shearing, **F** Vulcanizing, Mixing, **A** Cutting, Fitting, Lining, **C** Buttons, Threads, **T** Sewing Machines, **U** etc. **R I N G.**

M Cotton, Wool, Linen. **A** Leather, Silk, Straw, **T** Fur, Feathers, Rubber, **E** Felt, Fibre, Paper, **R** Wood, Pulp, etc. **I A L S.**

J Precious Stones, Rings, **E** Chains, Necklaces, **W** Bracelets, Pins, Brooches, **E** Pendants, Watches, Pocketbooks, **L** Accessories, Perfumeries, **R** Cosmetics. **Y E T C.**

M Advertising, Department **A** Stores, **R** Adding Machines, **K** Cash Registers, **E** etc. **T I N G.**

TRANSPORTATION

A Horses,   **V** Sleds, Chariots, **N** Camels, Oxen,   **E** Jinrikishas, Carts, Wagons, **I** Mules,   **H** Sleighs, Coaches, Hearses, **M** Llamas,   **I** Coffins, Carriages, Cabs, **A** Dogs,   **C** Velocipedes, Wheel-Barrows, **L** Burros,   **L** Trucks, Cars, Trams, **S** Elephants, etc.   **E** Tricycles,   **S** Bicycles, etc.

S Sandals, Snowshoes,   **R** Horse, Steam, **H** Skates, Roller-skates,   **A** Cable, Compressed, **O** Rubbers, Boots,   **I** Air Trolleys, **E** Gaiters, Slippers,   **L** Third-rail, Elevated, **S** Motor Skates, etc.   **R** Monorail, Alcohol,   **O** Motors, Gasoline   **A** Motors, Electric   **D**   **S** Motors, etc.

S Rail, Steam Propeller,   **H** Turbine, Submarine, **TELEPHONE** { Poles, Exchanges, Directories, Phonographs, Graphophones, etc. **I** Balloons, Dirigibles, **P** Aeroplanes, **S** Helicopters, etc.

TELEGRAPH { Wiring, Insulation, Batteries, Poles, Conduits, Semaphore, Stock Tickers, Switchboards, etc. **A** Steam, Gasoline, **U** Alcohol, **T** Electric, **O** Elevators, **S** Moving Stairways, etc.

M Envelopes, Stationery, **A** Postage, Expressage, **SUBWAYS AND TUBES** { Reinforced Concrete, Air-locks, etc. **I** Pneumatic Mail boxes, **L** Letter boxes, etc.

BANKING { Species, Banknotes, Vaults, and Safes, Checks, etc.
Copyright 1909, by Goodwin B. Smith.

CHAPTER VII.

NECESSARY STEPS

"In any business, it is to-day's unknown facts that wreck the machine tomorrow. Therefore, find out the facts."

Almost all inventors show an unusually needless amount of haste in rushing off to an attorney and applying for a patent, even before they have given their idea any practical demonstration whatsoever. This is, in the opinion of the writer, all wrong, and is not the most practical way to proceed. The application for patent, and filing of carefully drawn specification and claims, is, of course, highly important and necessary, but it should not be undertaken until after the most searching, practical tests of the invention, as well as the most careful investigation as to the *public demand* for your idea, as it is from the latter source that profits will come. The care with which your specification is written, and the claims drawn, will regulate the strength of your protection against infringers. Don't forget that the red seal and blue ribbon on a worthless patent are just as red and blue as they are on a high-grade, "suit-proof," one that has stood the tests of the courts from bottom to the top.

WHAT THE UNITED STATES SUPREME COURT SAYS.

"The specification and claims of a patent, particularly if the invention be at all complicated, constitute one of the most difficult legal instruments to draw with accuracy, and in view of the fact that valuable inventions are often placed in the hands of inexperienced persons to prepare such specification and claims, it is no matter of surprise that the latter frequently fail to describe with requisite certainty the exact invention of the patentee, and err either in claiming that which the patentee had not in fact patented, or in omitting some element which was a valuable or essential part of his actual invention." Topliff vs. Topliff, 145 U.S. 156.

The highest court of the land thus puts itself on record in reference to the importance of having the specification and claims of your patent properly drawn. It is equally as important to have your models, drawings, patterns, etc., accurately designed and executed.

Every week the "Official Gazette," published by the U.S. Patent Office, is chock full of new, novel and ingenious devices on which patents have been granted, but which are in lines in which the demand and sales are so very restricted that the profits in seventeen years will scarcely pay for the cost of the patent. As Dr. Grimshaw, Ph.D., M. E., a celebrated inventor and scholar, known to many Americans, and at present residing in Germany, so aptly puts it, it is well to remember "There are some lines in which competition is so fierce that there would not be any use in coming into the field. If the Marquis of Worcester, Watt, Fulton and Morse, Whitney and Howe, Edison and McCormick, and a dozen more of the great inventors of the world, past and present, were to put their heads together, and get up a new car-coupler, the chances are that they could not get thirty cents for the patent. The thing is overdone."

Many, many, hard-earned dollars are annually expended by inexperienced inventors in the building of ornate, nickel-plated models that from a practical, business stand-point are commercially impossible, and never will amount to anything. While they are splendid in "theory," and pretty to look at, and talk about, yet in "practice" and real utility they are of no value. Don't go to the expense of a model until you know your device is patentable, mechanically practicable, commercially salable, and in demand in the markets of the world, and in a class in which there is no killing competition.

Caveats have proven to be, oftentimes, worse than worthless. The Government fee is $10; the attorney fee from $10 to $25. When you file your application you are notified by the U.S. Patent Office of an interference suit, if someone else happens to file an application along similar lines. It is then "up to you" to show that "you thought of it first," usually a very expensive and disappointing task. Don't apply for a caveat, is the writer's advice.

Confidence is the bed-rock foundation of all business today, so don't be afraid of anyone trying to steal your idea. A simple and inexpensive means to follow is to have a rough pencil sketch and description of your idea, dated and signed by yourself and two competent witnesses. Then, if the question of priority of invention is raised, you have a strong document to substantiate your claims to priority.

If your idea will pass muster on the Six Cardinal Tests, (1) as regards patentability; (2) as regards mechanical practicability; (3) as regards its possession of superior merit and low cost of production; (4) as regards a large and constant public demand for it; (5) as regards to its being better, cheaper and more salable than similar devices already on the market; (6) as regards to the competition it will encounter,—then, and only then, are you justified in spending time and money in applying for a patent, and having proper working model built, etc. Don't rely on your own judgment in such matters,—it is of necessity greatly prejudiced, and rightly so. You, as an inventor, are in the same relative position as the mother of a new baby. Both of you undoubtedly feel that your offspring possesses all the graces, and has no bad points whatsoever. But your invention does not have as good a show, at least no better, than the new baby has of developing into a "world-beater" or prodigy. In both instances it will require careful development, much study, and the hardest kind of work to make a moderate success of the new infant. Another point to remember is that the one who is responsible for its successful development is entitled to more credit and greater rewards than the father of the idea or infant.

A Patent Attorney, must, of very necessity, be disposed to find practically everything submitted to him "to be patentable." Some firms go so far as to mail their guarantees that ideas are patentable, but your idea has five other points in which it may "fall down." Mere patentability is only one-sixth of the necessary ground you must cover. Your friends may think you are a genius, a wonder, and you may be, but don't let their adulation turn your head to the extent of your forgetting the six tests necessary to your idea's success. If you are sick, you go to the best physician you can find; if your horse is sick, you send for a veterinarian; if you are required to go to Court, you retain a good lawyer to represent your side,—you don't try to cure yourself, or your horse, or defend yourself. You go to a specialist in these lines. Follow the same sane method in your patent matters. The "no-cure-no-pay" doctor is not highly regarded, neither are patent firms that do a "contingent fee" business on the "no patent-no pay" basis. Cut rates are also to be shunned. Good service demands and can exact commensurate returns. Economy in these matters is a poor policy to pursue.

Analysis of the Six Cardinal Patent Tests.

"If I am building a mountain, and stop before the last bucketful of earth is placed on the summit, I have failed."—Confucius.

First: Would it be possible to cover my idea or invention by a good, strong, basic patent?

First and foremost, the thing to do is to find out if your invention can be properly covered by a good, strong patent,—a basic patent, if possible, and if not basic, at least, one covering some novel elements which would prevent unscrupulous imitators and dealers from substituting "something just as good" for your invention. In this connection we might say that any bright attorney can find some way in which an alleged patent can be issued practically on anything, so very little dependence can be placed, as a rule, on "preliminary searches" that are furnished "free of cost." Expect to pay at least $5.00 for it, and ask for the references the search develops. We place the covering of an invention by strong letters patent first, as we consider it of the utmost importance that an invention, to be a commercial success, must grant its owner a virtual monopoly.

Second: Is my invention mechanically practicable?

There are a great many ideas which of themselves are good, and still are not of themselves of any value. It is of equal importance, in order to make a success of an invention, to have it conform to certain recognized mechanical principles, and capable of economical production through the regular trade and manufacturing channels. In other words, an invention nowadays would be seriously handicapped if it was necessary to revolutionize the present equipment of factories to bring it out.

(In this connection it might be interesting to note that Thomas A. Edison, in an article published in "The Star," of Washington, September 17th, 1908, said that in his opinion Wright Brothers were working on the wrong principle with their flying machine. In Edison's opinion the machine should not be dependent on the skill of the operator, but should be capable of automatic operation somewhat similar to an automobile or the locomotive.)

Third: Can my invention be more cheaply manufactured than similar devices already on the market?

If your invention will enter the markets of the world in close competition with other devices of similar nature, it is necessary that it possesses the possibility for lower cost of production than the articles it will meet in competition. If it costs more to make, it will be heavily handicapped from the start. If it costs less to make it will have this additional advantage pulling in its favor from the start.

Fourth: Does my idea possess conspicuous novelty and superior merit over similar devices already on the market?

The established, advertised article in the markets of the world always has a great advantage over new and relatively untried devices. A new article, to succeed, must show at a glance that it is "something better." In addition to that, it must have superior merit which will at once make it possible to bring about a quick sale in competition with the article already on the market. If your invention is better, costs less to produce, has more "talking points," dealers will be quick to buy it. Otherwise, possibly not.

Fifth: Is there a large, constant, public demand for my invention, or its product?

Public demand for anyone's invention practically regulates its success, from a commercial standpoint. If there is no public demand for it, there can be no individual profit derived from it. In other words, it is useless to apply for a patent on any art, machine or process where the demand for its use is very limited. For instance, it would be ridiculous to patent a process for performing one single act or function, the demand for which would cease as soon as the act or function was accomplished. To illustrate, some years ago, while building the City Hall, in Philadelphia, it was necessary to raise the enormous statue of William Penn to the top of the tower. This was quite an undertaking, and a great many bright men cudgeled their brains as to the best means of accomplishing the result. It would have been very foolish to patent the means by which the statue was put on the top of the tower, because after it was placed on the top there would be no further demand for the process or means by which Penn was raised to his elevated position.

"Little and often fills the purse" is a familiar quotation to many of us, and is especially applicable to the profits to be made from inventions.

Sixth: Is there killing competition in the class to which my invention belongs?

If your device is likely to run into a section of the trade of the world where questionable tactics and high-pressure methods are necessary to keep one's head above water, our advice to you would be, "Don't do it!" as it would possibly be better to "follow the lines of least resistance," and spend your time and money on something where you would have a better chance for success.

In the year 1909, what chances do you think an inventor would have in starting a business in competition with the United States Steel Corporation, or the American Sugar Refining Company, or the Standard Oil Company, or the Pennsylvania Railroad Company, or the Paper Trust, or the Bell Telephone Company, or the Moving Picture Trust, or the American Can Company, or the Baldwin Locomotive Works? These enormous aggregations of brains and capital would make it quixotic to attempt to compete with them in the markets of the world. Yet you may be able to invent something they would be glad to purchase!

If your patent is weak or deficient in any one of these six cardinal tests it is heavily handicapped to just that extent in the race for success. Do not depend on your own judgment, as your judgment is naturally prejudiced, and will not, most likely, reflect a dependable forecast of the public attitude toward your invention. It will be cheaper in the long run to get reliable counsel in these respects before you start, rather than learning it from bitter experience.

THE UNITED STATES CAPITOL.

Terse Suggestions

This is the day of short cuts. If you take the long way 'round, you will never "arrive." Cuts, to be short, need not be poorly done with a blunt knife. The cleverest surgeon is he who can perform the biggest operation in the shortest time. Learn to do things quickly, but do them well.

In this hustling world we must "get there," and "get there quick," not only in our conversation but in all our work. We must avoid non-essentials.

Spend your time and money on money-savers rather than on frills. Do your work under a system, and stick to it. Do not have a too elaborate system, however.

With the machine work of the Twentieth Century method, fine hand work is now considered a luxury.

Don't beat about the bush. Get right down to the point. The swiftest road to success has the fewest curves.

"Dost thou love life? Then do not squander time, for that is the stuff life is made of."—Franklin.

CHAPTER VIII.

SOUNDING THE MARKET

"People are always to be found who think anything with which they are not familiar cannot be good."

If the average inventor goes out among his friends with his invention and asks them their opinion of it, he will hear some such expressions as this: "Old man, you are a marvel!"; "You will be a millionaire some day, sure thing!"; "That looks a big winner!"; "Beats anything I ever saw!" and so on. But such comments are absolutely worthless. Many an inventor's head has been turned by just such praise. It is all well-meant, best-intentioned, and highly gratifying, but as an indication of what will be likely to happen to your invention it is worse than valueless. It is grossly misleading. Your friends want to encourage you, help you. They see only your invention's good points, not its vital weaknesses. They are not "skilled in the art,"—are not in a position to judge competently at all. Do not depend on any such opinions. Go to a specialist in such lines. Will a stranger to you buy your invention in preference to the ones already on the market? If so, he exacts a lower price or a better article, which amount to the same thing. Can you manufacture your invention and sell it at a good profit in competition with others? Will the wholesalers handle it? Can they do so at a good profit? Has it good selling and talking points, or do you need to make excuses for it? Is the field now over-crowded? In this connection, remember the "Six Cardinal Patent Tests," especially the fifth and sixth. Is there a large, constant, public demand for my invention or its product? And is there killing competition in the class to which my invention belongs? Get the advice of a specialist.

CHAPTER IX.

PRACTICAL DEVELOPMENT

"Everything in this world is a development. Nothing happens by chance."

Can my invention be made to do better work by putting in gears in place of that sprocket chain? Would canvas be cheaper and better than leather in that belt? Won't a cotter pin be cheaper and better in place of that nut? Won't a steel casting be cheaper and better than that expensive machined steel bearing? Would not my machine do better work and cost less if I stuck to just this one operation?

Questions such as this you must ask yourself. The successful inventor is not a "one-idea" man. He must be on the watch for "something better" all the time, until he and his expert advisers are convinced by *actual tests* in *actual service* that it is absolutely right in every way. No invention is complete and perfect when it is first conceived. Its successful development is a series of changes, substitutions, alterations, rearrangements, until finally it attains marketable shape.

At a meeting of mechanical experts in Philadelphia one evening, six men were asked the very best way to make a certain piece of machine work. There were six different answers.—"Many men of many minds."—Which was the best way, and why? If you take your own ideas you will possibly have but one way to do it, and your way may not prove the best way in the end. The successful invention of today dominates its particular field. Why? Because it is better than others.

Successful development of any invention requires a great degree of patience, unlimited hard work, belief in ultimate success, and competent theoretical and practical knowledge of mechanics, physics, mathematics, salesmanship, shop practice and the like. It is a science in itself.

"Whatever I have tried to do in life, I have tried with all my heart to do well; whatever I have devoted myself to, I have devoted myself to completely; in great aims and small I have always been thoroughly in earnest."—Charles Dickens.

CHAPTER X.

LOWER COST SUPERIOR MERIT

"An idea of itself may be good, but still not of itself be of any value."

Patents, to meet with even moderate commercial success, must be on a "human necessity" or "luxury"—must cost less and be better than the ones already on the market. That is this whole chapter in a nutshell. Lines upon lines could be said about it, but the reader will grasp the point.

CHAPTER XI.

APPLICATION

FOR PATENTS, DESIGN PATENTS, TRADE-MARKS LABELS AND COPYRIGHTS

"The man who does things is the man who is doing things. The busiest man in the city is the man who is always ready for new business."

"To postpone action generally means an attempt to kill by time."—John Timothy Stone.

What is Patentable.

An art or process,

Machines or mechanisms,

Manufactured articles,

Compositions of matter,

Improvements on any of the above,

if the art, machine, manufactured article, composition of matter, or improvement thereof, for which a Patent is desired, was not known or used by others, in this country, and has not been patented or described in any printed publication in this or any foreign country, before the applicant's invention or discovery thereof, and has not been in public use or on sale for more than two years prior to his application, unless the same is proved to have been abandoned.

Usual Cost

The cost of taking out a patent varies with different cases. In a simple case such as, for instance, an improvement in potato mashers, it is, ordinarily,

$65. Some attorneys charge $5 less, and some $10 more, according to their schedule. This amount is made up as follows:

Preliminary search of Patent Office records $ 5 00 Preparation of drawings, one sheet   5 00 Preparation of specification and claims   20 00 First Government fee   15 00 Final Government fee, payable six months after allowance of patent   20 00 Total cost of simple one-sheet case $ 65 00

Complicated machines and processes that require a large number of sheets of drawings and contain a great deal of detail work cost often times, especially if interferences develop, as much as $1000. Elsewhere in this volume is quoted the opinion of the Supreme Court as regards the importance of having the specification and claims carefully drawn. Have your work done well, and expect to pay a fair price for good service.

Design Patents. Preparation of drawings and specification, and prosecuting case $ 25 00 Government fee, for 3½ $ 10 00 Government fee, for 7 $ 15 00 Government fee, for 14 $ 30 00   Copyrights. The cost of obtaining a Copyright, including all fees, is usually $ 5 00   Trade-marks. Preliminary Search, Government and Attorney's Fees $ 25 00   Labels. Government and Attorney's Fees $ 16 00   Note.—Patents run for seventeen years, and cannot be renewed. Design Patents run for 3½, 7 or 14 years, as the case may be. Trademarks run for thirty years, and longer, if desired. Label Patents run for 28 years, and may be renewed for fourteen years longer, if desired. Copyrights run for 28 years, and may be renewed for fourteen years longer, if desired. Special rates and terms are payable on "Interferences," Infringements, Appeals and Assignments.

Foreign Patents can be procured in all civilized countries, but should be applied for only after the most careful study as to whether they are likely to prove profitable to the inventor. We are inclined to say it is the exception when they do.

"Rules of Practice" issued by the United States Patent Office contain the following in regard to the importance of care in the selection of an attorney:

"As the value of Patents depends largely upon the careful preparation of the Specification and Claims, the assistance of competent counsel will, in most instances, be of advantage to the applicant; but the value of their services will be proportionate to their skill and honesty, and too much care cannot be exercised in their selection."

"Before you spend much money, either your own or any one's else, be sure (1) that your invention will work; (2) that no one else has patented it; (3) that there is an opportunity for its sale; (4) that there is not too much competition. Many a man starts off and orders a fancy nickel-plated model, and applies for his patent, only to find that the idea will not work even the least little bit. In this matter the advice of some one else well up in the theory, added to that of some one else well up in the practice, would be valuable."

"Many an application done up in all the bravery of typewriting, notarial seal, and all that, has been rejected like a bad penny for the very simple reason that some one else had before patented the idea, or something enough like it to bar out the newcomer. It is cheaper to have the ground gone over first by a preliminary search by a competent person even before the application is written out."

"Don't be unduly suspicious. Don't fear that any one who takes more than a passing interest in your invention is going to steal it. All business is based more or less on trust. You trust some one every day. So does every one else. There is no use in your showing every Tom, Dick and Harry what you have, or expect to have; but if you show a man anything at all, do it with trust. If he is not trustworthy, do not show him anything."—Dr. Grimshaw.

CHAPTER XII.

MARKETING

"Anybody can slide down hill, but it takes good legs and good wind to go up."—Silent Partner.

The brightest minds of the business world are endeavoring to solve the problem of how best to market an article. Of course, unlimited capital, and a good article greatly lessen the problem. But to start with little or no money, build up a business, equip the plant, buy raw materials, hire help, manage a factory, establish credit, advertise, fill orders, collect accounts, and do the thousand and one other things necessary to make success of a business requires a good, virile mind, and plenty of hard work and close attention to detail, and should be a steady, gradual development. With honesty of purpose, quality of product, absolute fair-dealing, push and untiring energy as guides, any man or woman given good health, common sense and a fairly meritorious patented article can unquestionably succeed in profitably marketing it. A steady climb with unflagging zeal and singleness of purpose always win out. The motto should be, "This one thing I do."

It has been found from experience that it is usually well to get the best expert advice in connection with the establishment of a new business before making plans for spending much money. There are specialists in all business lines today, and as a rule it proves to be wise economy to spend money in payment of their services.

Some of the largest industrial establishments in the world are the direct outgrowth of a very small plant judiciously handled and energetically developed. Of course, in marketing a product, one must know exactly what the product costs. Allow proper margin for management expenses, fixed charges, depreciation, selling expenses and the like. It is usually safe to add one hundred per cent. to the manufacturing cost for the purpose of covering administrative and fixed charges. Wholesale selling prices should always conform to the list put out by other manufacturers. In other words,

An article retailing at 5 c usually sells wholesale for 35 c to 40 c doz. An article retailing at 10 c usually sells wholesale for 60 c to 90 c doz. An article

47

retailing at 25 c usually sells wholesale for $1.75 to $2.25 doz. An article retailing at 50 c usually sells wholesale for $3.50 to $4.50 doz. An article retailing at $1.00 usually sells wholesale for $7.50 to $9.00 doz. The gross prices are approximately as follows:

On a 5 c article, $4.20 to $4.80 per gross On a 10 c article, $7.20 to $9.80 per gross On a 25 c article, $21.00 to $27.00 per gross On a 50 c article, $42.00 to $54.00 per gross On a $1.00 article, $90.00 to $108.00 per gross It is usually customary to give a discount of from 5 per cent. to 10 per cent., if ordered in gross lots. Terms of settlement show considerable variation in different lines, and range anywhere from 1 per cent. to 8 per cent. for cash in ten days, with extension of credit of from thirty days net to ninety days "extra dating." There are some splendid books advertised and published along these lines which can be had from the various publishers. There are also weekly and monthly periodicals that will prove of great benefit to anyone engaging in a new business.

Carefully prepared catalogues, stationery, printed matters, follow-up letters, etc., should be used. Consult a specialist about these matters.

"The world always listens to a man with a will in him."

CHAPTER XIII.

DISCOURAGEMENTS AND DANGERS

When to-day's difficulties overshadow yesterday's triumphs and obscure the bright visions of tomorrow—

When plans upset, and whole years of effort seem to crystallize into a single hour of concentrated bitterness—

When little annoyances eat into the mind's very quick, and corrode the power to view things calmly—

When the jolts of misfortune threaten to jar loose the judgment from its moorings—

Remember that in every business, in every career, there are valleys to cross, as well as hills to scale, that every mountain range of hope is broken by chasms of discouragement through which run torrent streams of despair!

To quit in the chasms is to fail. See always in your mind's eye those sunny summits of success!

Don't quit in the chasm! Keep on!"—System.

A careful study of the histories of great inventors and inventions impresses the student most forcibly with the glaring fact that while the field of invention offers, and has paid, fabulously large rewards to the fortunate genius who invents or discovers some really new device or idea, it also is a field full of discouragements, dangers and heart-breaking delays, disappointments and unfulfilled hopes, to say nothing of time and energy utterly wasted by misguided zeal and misdirected effort. We need to look at the matter from all angles, and study to avoid the pitfalls and dangers history unerringly points out to us, as well as learn thoroughly the lesson so dearly bought for us by the noble men and women in the army of inventors who have gone before.

The following table shows the startlingly large totals of Patents and Re-issues issued by the United States Government since the year 1837, up to last year, 1908:

1837 435 1855 2013 1873 12864 1891 23244 1838 520 1856 2505 1874 13599 1892 23559 1839 425 1857 2896 1875 14837 1893 23769 1840 473 1858 3710 1876 15595 1894 20867 1841 495 1859 4538 1877 14187 1895 22057 1842 517 1860 4819 1878 13444 1896 23373 1843 519 1861 3340 1879 13213 1897 23794 1844 497 1862 3521 1880 13947 1898 22267 1845 503 1863 4170 1881 16584 1899 25527 1846 638 1864 5020 1882 19267 1900 26499 1847 569 1865 6616 1883 22383 1901 27373 1848 653 1866 9450 1884 20413 1902 27886 1849 1077 1867 13015 1885 24233 1903 31699 1850 993 1868 13378 1886 22508 1904 30934 1851 872 1869 13986 1887 21477 1905 30399 1852 1019 1870 13321 1888 20506 1906 31965 1853 961 1871 13033 1889 24158 1907 36620 1854 1844 1872 13590 1890 26292 1908 32757

The United States Government has issued, approximately, 900,000 PATENTS. When we compare the number of patents that have proven to be commercial successes (in other words, money-makers), how pitifully small the list is by comparison! How many "blasted hopes," vanishing "air castles"; how much poverty, how many wrecked homes, how many suicides (but why prolong this list?) are represented by those Letters Patent that did not win! Why did they fail? The seal was just as red, the ribbon just as blue, they cost just as much, the drawings were just as clear—then why did they fail?

For one, any or all of the following reasons:

1. The claims were weak.

2. The invention would not work.

3. The cost of manufacture was too great.

4. The idea was feebly patentable, but not sufficiently new or novel.

5. There was no demand for it.

6. The big fellows froze it out!

Or, to be exact, they failed to stand the SIX CARDINAL TESTS given elsewhere.

Don't intend to "take up inventing," as some men say, and expect to make a success of it, without any preparation, with little practical education, much less diligent study. You can't do it, unless it be by merest accident! Look at history. She tells the story so that all can hear and heed it. Think of Edison's perseverance, his all-night experiments, without food or drink, his life-long hard and unremitting effort. Picture George Stephenson's disappointments; the silly opposition he met; his constant "if at first you don't succeed, try, try again!" spirit! Think of John Fitch and his steamboat; Ottmar Mergenthaler and his linotype,—years of trial and study; remember Fulton and his "Clermont"; the Wright Brothers, Wilbur and Orville, working year after year, planning, perfecting, always at it! Success in invention is not "easy money."—It does not consist of "thinking out an idea," picking up a magazine or paper and reading a Patent advertisement "Free Report as to Patentability,"—"No Patent No Pay,"—"Send sketch," etc., etc.; drawing a rough pencil sketch and forwarding it to the attorneys the inventor picked out; getting back a mysterious looking certificate done up in purple ink, seals, etc., purporting to guarantee that the idea is a patentable one, or he doesn't pay a cent. Next he forwards from $40 to $50 and gets back the specification and claims (the claims "claiming" every thing above the earth, and numbering possibly twenty to fifty) for his oath and signature. Then the case is filed with the Patent Office. After waiting anywhere from six months to several years the attorney notifies him that his case is "allowed" (sometimes it is rejected, and he has thrown his money away), and will be issued upon payment of the final Government fee of $20, that is, of course, provided it has not run into an "interference." If it has, it is to be regretted, as it may mean the loss of all the inventor's money in fees and expenses, and the loss of his case in the end. But for the sake of the story we'll say he gets his patent in a big, official looking envelope. He sees his name on it, the seal, the ribbon, the picture of the Patent Office, and his heart and head naturally swell with pride. But if he looks at it carefully, he will find the claims (and they are what count) consist of one big long paragraph of several hundred words, without a period in it, describing the exact or fancied construction, the protection in the claim being

51

so restricted and limited in scope that a poor chauffeur could drive a sight-seeing auto through the alleged Patent without touching sides, top or bottom! The twenty to fifty claims were all rejected. Then what happens? He shows it to his family, friends, neighbors. He gets his name in the town paper. He is spoken of as an "Inventor." Then he begins to wonder what he is going to do with it. He is dreaming possibly of millions, when it is not worth cents.

When his name appears in the Official Gazette he will begin getting circulars, cunningly worded letters, postal cards, etc., mentioning his wonderful (?) invention (it may be a new paring knife!) and saying that for any amount ranging from $1.00 to $30.00 the writer will be glad to sell the patent for any amount their fertile imagination may conjure up, always more than ample, but after the money is sent for "advertising," "printing," or what not, all signs of a sale absolutely disappear. (Don't send any money to a firm to sell your patent unless they are known to be reliable and trustworthy, and *don't guarantee* to do anything but treat you fairly and make an honest effort to sell it.) The safe and rational way is to test your idea thoroughly in advance of having it patented, and then you are practically sure of a sale.

Here is the moral: Some day he will wake up and find he might better have painted the house with the $65, or given it to his wife for a new dress. He will give up the idea of fame and fortune so alluringly set forth in the circulars sent out by some attorneys.

This is an every-day case one in the business meets with all the time. It is all wrong, but is only too true. Authorities state that 90 per cent. of the patents issued today are worthless from a commercial standpoint! Statistics appear to prove it, although it is hard to get at the real facts. The reader may feel that the author is trying to discourage inventors from entering the field. No. All that is intended is to show and point out the rational course to pursue in applying for Patents and endeavoring to be a success as an inventor. Volumes could be written on this subject, but the above will serve as an average example of blasted hopes and misdirected effort.

"Failure is only endeavor temporarily off the track. How foolish it would be to abandon it in the ditch."

BRIGHT SIDE

The output of all the gold, silver and diamond mines in the world does not equal in value the profits earned from American inventions.

Probably between fifty and sixty millions of dollars have been, spent in procuring patents issued by the United States Government, on the basis that the average patent costs from $60 to $65, and there have been 900,000 issued. To show that patents are profitable, we need only recall the fact that almost twice this amount has been received in profits from several of them, namely, the Bell Telephone, for instance, or the Harvester, Sewing Machine, Telegraph, Phonograph, etc. Authorities on the subject are of the opinion that there are almost two hundred patents in force in the United States today that return profits of over one million dollars per year; several hundred that return half-a-million dollars profit; five or six hundred that return from $250,000 to $500,000 in profits; and an enormous number which return incomes of from $5,000 to $100,000 annually.

Inventive genius can exact the highest possible price, for its labor in the markets of the world. If you are a genius you cannot employ your time to better advantage than in endeavoring to improve methods at present in use, or invent combinations that will cheapen production, or discover new elements or combinations that will effect economic results. The history of inventions, poets, past and present, tell us that success is possible, if persistently pursued. Do not allow the dangers and discouragements that we must all meet with to dishearten you. As Longfellow so beautifully puts it:

"Be still, sad heart! and cease repining; Behind the clouds is the sun still shining; Thy fate is the common fate of all, Into each life some rain must fall, Some days must be dark and dreary."

CHAPTER XIV.

SELLING PATENTS

It is not so much how you sell your patent. It is what you get for it.

Patents can be disposed of in various ways. We are sorry to say that the majority of patents issued today, for reasons already stated, are disposed of on the scrap heap, or the waste basket. However, if you have a patent that possesses commercial value, it can possibly be disposed of in one of the following manners:

First, by selling it outright for a cash consideration.

Second, by selling state, county or shop rights for the use of your invention.

Third, by placing it with an already established concern on a royalty basis.

Fourth, by the organization of a company or partnership for its production and marketing.

Taking up each one of the methods in order, the following explanations will possibly be of interest:

It has often been said that an inventor rarely underestimates the value of his patent. Associating with and meeting large numbers of inventors from time to time has convinced the writer that no one individual can give a reliable estimate of the value of anyone's invention. If an inventor desires to sell his invention outright, he should take into consideration, in fixing the price, just how much he spent on the development of the idea; how much money he actually spent in procuring the patent, building the models, and getting the invention into marketable shape. He should add a certain modest percentage for good will, and if he desires to sell outright, base his figures on some such estimates. For instance, a small, simple patent could be estimated as being worth, say $2500 cash, as follows:

Twenty weeks of time spent in developing the idea, $25 per week $ 500 00 Procurement of patent   75 00 Building of models   150 00 Expert advice and counsel   25 00 Manufactured samples, dies, tools, etc.   250 00 Good will, or present value of the patent per se   <u>1,500 00</u> Fair selling price for patent in which the time, labor, expenditures, etc., were approximately in accordance with the figures listed above, would be $ 2,500 00   The man that buys the patent will be entitled to a great deal more profit than the inventor who conceived it, and by the time he has it on the market and has the sale established, he will be entitled to everything he earns. Of course, there are exceptions to every rule, but the writer is not speaking of exceptions now.

Another very profitable way to dispose of a patent is the selling of state, county and shop rights. This has brought many inventors very large returns, although it involves a good deal of selling expense, and salesmanship of the highest order.

The placing of a patent on a royalty basis, and the payment of a nominal cash "*quid pro quo*" we consider the best method of disposing of an invention, and the one most likely to prove profitable, provided, of course, that the firm with which the patent is placed is thoroughly reliable, and can energetically push its sale. Elsewhere in this volume you have read of the enormous sums in royalties that have been received on various successful inventions. One particular illustration at this time may not be in-apropos.

Oscar Hammerstein, the New York theatre proprietor, sold his first cigar-making machine for $6,000 cash. The next one he invented he placed on a royalty, and made $250,000. This is almost a typical case.

When the patent or its product has a sufficiently large public demand it is oftentimes better to organize a new company for its development and sale. This is done by applying for a charter under some favorable State laws, (it is usually expedient to apply in the State in which it is intended to manufacture,) and give the inventor a reasonable stock interest in the company, together with an executive position if he is capable of filling it.

"You must bear some of the burden of introduction yourself. A capitalist may be willing to bet his hard dollars that your idea will work, if you have secured a patent; or he may be induced to bet that it is patentable, if you show him that it will work; but moneyed men who will bet that your invention is both patentable and practicable are few and far between. If they make such a bet, it will be with very heavy odds against the inventor."—Grimshaw.

Do not forget that some men have made millions out of a single patent. Do not forget that others have lost all they could make and borrow.

"Victories that are easy are cheap. Those only are worth having which come as a result of hard fighting."

CHAPTER XV.

CONCLUSION

The old adage, "Be sure you are right and then go ahead," is especially apropos advice to inventors. But how can you be SURE you *are* right? Only by investigation that is strictly impersonal and unprejudiced in every sense. You can have this work of investigation done for you—you can buy advice of this kind just as you can buy legal or medical advice from specialists. Better disburse $25 or $50 in procuring sound expert advice than spend weeks, months and years chasing a mirage or will-o'-wisp. You are not compelled to accept the advice if it differs from your ideas, but you will most likely learn a great deal that will pay you handsomely.

The writer is fully aware that this line of talk is opposed to the "don't hesitate," "send at once," "delays are dangerous," "the other fellow will get ahead of you" arguments so generally used by individuals who "have an axe to grind." BE SURE you are right, and then go ahead—don't THINK you are sure—BE SURE!

The author feels that a careful weighing of all statements and facts in this volume will be of great value to anyone considering the application for a patent. History has undoubtedly proven that *good* patents are possibly more profitable than any other investment that can be made. If you have an idea, or have made a discovery that you think will prove of benefit to mankind, the wise and prudent course is to have it thoroughly investigated, in all points as relate to its success. The small cost of a reliable investigation would be money well spent as it is possible your idea or discovery may be the means of bringing you in enormous wealth.

CHAPTER XVI.

STATISTICS OF THE COUNTRIES OF THE WORLD

COUNTRIES POPULATION SQ. MILES CAPITALS China 426,447,000 4,218,401 Peking. British Empire1 396,968,798 11,146,084 London. Russian Empire 129,004,514 8,660,395 St. Petersburg. United States2 76,303,887 3,602,990 Washington. United States and islands3 89,000,000 3,756,884 Washington. France and colonies 65,166,967 3,250,000 Paris. German Empire, in Europe 58,549,000 208,830 Berlin. Austro-Hungarian Empire 46,973,359 264,595 Vienna. Japan 44,260,604 147,669 Tokio. Netherlands and Colonies 33,042,238 778,187 The Hague. Turkish Empire 33,559,787 1,652,533 Constantinople. Italy 32,449,754 110,665 Rome. Spain 17,550,216 196,173 Madrid. Brazil 18,000,000 3,218,130 Rio Janeiro. Mexico 13,546,500 767,316 City of Mexico. Korea 10,519,000 85,000 Seoul. Congo State 8,000,000 802,000 .... Persia 7,653,600 636,000 Teheran. Portugal and colonies 11,073,681 951,785 Lisbon. Sweden and Norway 7,376,321 297,321 .... Belgium 6,069,321 11,373 Brussels. Argentine Republic 4,800,000 1,095,013 Buenos Ayres. Chile 3,110,085 256,860 Santiago. Peru 3,000,000 405,040 Lima. Switzerland 3,312,551 15,981 Berne. Greece 2,433,806 24,977 Athens. Denmark 2,417,441 14,780 Copenhagen. Venezuela 2,444,816 566,159 Caracas. Liberia 2,060,000 35,000 Monrovia. Cuba 1,600,000 44,000 Havana. Guatemala 1,574,340 46,774 N. Guatemala. Hayti 1,211,625 9,830 Port au Prince. Paraguay 600,000 145,000 Asuncion. Panama 285,000 31,571 Panama.   POPULATION OF THE UNITED STATES.

Alabama 1,828,697 Montana 243,329 Alaska 63,592 Nebraska 1,066,300 Arizona 122,931 Nevada 42,335 Arkansas 1,311,564 New Hampshire 411,588 California 1,485,053 New Jersey 1,883,699 Colorado 539,700 New Mexico 195,310 Connecticut 908,420 New York 7,268,894 Dakota .... North Carolina 1,893,810 Delaware 184,735 North Dakota 319,146 District of Columbia 278,718 Ohio 4,157,545 Florida 528,542 Oklahoma 398,331 Georgia 2,216,331 Oregon 413,536 Hawaii 154,001 Pennsylvania 6,302,115 Idaho 161,772 Rhode Island 428,556 Illinois 4,821,550 South Carolina

1,340,310 Indiana 2,516,462 South Dakota 401,570 Indian Territory 392,060 Tennessee 2,020,616 Iowa 2,231,853 Texas 3,048,710 Kansas 1,470,495 Utah 276,749 Kentucky 2,147,174 Vermont 343,641 Louisiana 1,381,625 Virginia 1,854,184 Maine 694,466 Washington 518,103 Maryland 1,188,044 West Virginia 958,800 Massachusetts 2,805,346 Wisconsin 2,069,042 Michigan 2,420,982 Wyoming   92,531 Minnesota 1,751,394   Mississippi 1,551,270   Total 76,303,387 Missouri 3,106,665   Population Continental United States (including Alaska), 76,149,386 (1900); Philippines, 8,000,000; Porto Rico, 953,233; Hawaii, 154,001; Guam, 8,661; American Samoa, 5,800; Total population, 85,271,093. Population, 1904, estimating Continental United States, about 90,000,000.

1 These estimates of the population and area include the recently acquired great possessions in Africa. 2 Census of 1900. 3 Estimated for January 1st, 1904.

CHAPTER XVII.

MECHANICAL MOVEMENTS

In deciding upon the construction of models and the development of an idea, the proper mechanical movements should always be very carefully taken into consideration. In other words, movements which simplify the invention, minimize friction, and add power, are always to be preferred to clumsy and inefficient means or methods. Every inventor, and all students of the mechanical arts and sciences, should arrange any mechanism which they may desire to produce with the least number of parts possible, and embracing the greatest amount of simplicity of action.

On the following pages you will find a large number of mechanical movements with suitable description thereof which will undoubtedly assist inventors in developing and constructing their models of ideas. Most of the movements embraced in the following pages have appeared in various scientific journals and publications devoted to scientific and mechanical art. Study all the various movements applicable to your invention before deciding upon any particular one.

Mechanical Movements   1. Illustrating the transmission of power by simple pulleys and an open belt. The pulleys in this case rotate in the same direction.

2. Illustrating the transmission of power by simple pulleys and a crossed belt. The pulleys rotate in opposite directions.

3. Showing the transmission of motion from one shaft to another at right angles to it by means of guide-pulleys. There are two guide-pulleys side by side, one for each leaf of the belt.

4. Showing the transmission of motion from one shaft to another at right angles to it, without the use of guide-pulleys.

5. Showing a method of engaging, disengaging, and reversing the upright shaft on the left. The belt is shown on a loose pulley, and accordingly no motion is communicated to the shafts. If the belt be traversed on to the left-hand pulley, which is fast to the outer hollow shaft (b), motion is

communicated to the vertical shaft by the bevel-wheels How To Succeed and C; and if it be traversed on to the right-hand pulley, which is fast to the inner shaft (*a*), motion in an opposite direction is transmitted to the vertical shaft by the bevel-gear A and C.

6. Stepped speed-pulleys (on the left of the figure), used in lathes and machine-tools, and cone pulleys (on the right of the figure), used in cotton machinery, &c., for varying speed according to the requirements of the work being done. For a given speed of the upper shaft the speed of the lower one will be greater the more to the left the belt is placed. The cone-pulleys permit of more gradation in speed than the stepped arrangement.

7. Spur-gearing. The wheels rotate in opposite directions (cf. 12). The smaller wheel has the greater speed of revolution, and the speeds of the wheels are in the inverse ratio of their diameters.

8. Evans' variable friction gear. The gripping medium by which motion is transmitted from one cone to the other is a loose leather band, whose position can be varied by the hand-screw shown.

9. Bevel-gearing. This is an adaptation of the spur-wheel principle to the case of non-parallel axes.

10. A worm or endless screw geared with a worm wheel.

Mechanical Movements   11. Elliptical spur-gearing, used when a rotary motion of varying speed is required.

12. A spur-wheel geared internally with a pinion. The wheels rotate in the same direction (cf. 7).

13. Spur-gearing with oblique teeth, giving a more continuous bearing than 7.

14. Showing the transmission of power by rolling contact from one shaft to another obliquely situated with regard to it.

15. Different kinds of gearing for transmitting motion from one shaft to another arranged obliquely to it.

16. Two kinds of universal joints.

17. A method of transmitting motion from one shaft (the vertical) to another (the horizontal) by means of bevel-gearing, with a double-clutch for altering the direction of rotation. The bevel-wheels on the horizontal shaft are loose, and the direction of movement is determined by the side upon

which the double-clutch is engaged. The clutch slides upon a key or feather fixed on the shaft.

18. Transmission of two speeds by gearing. The hand is shown on the loose left hand pulley of the lower three. When it is moved on to the middle pulley, which is keyed to the shaft carrying the small pinion, a slow motion is transmitted to the lowest shaft; but when, it is on the right-hand pulley, which is fast to the outer shaft carrying the large spur-wheel, a quick speed is transmitted.

19. Transmission of two speeds by means of belts. The two outer pulleys on the lower shaft are loose, the two inner fast. With the belts arranged as shown, the speed of the lower shaft is slower than when both are traversed to the right.

Mechanical Movements   20. An intermittent circular motion in the direction indicated by the arrow is transmitted to the wheel A, by means of the oscillating rod D and the pawl B, from the reciprocating rectilinear motion of the rod C.

21. The continuous rotation of the shaft carrying the two cams or wipers gives to the rod A an intermittent alternating rectilinear motion. The rod is raised by the action of a wiper on the projection B, and it falls by its own weight. This contrivance is used in ore-stampers or pulverizers, power-hammers, &c.

22. The reciprocating rectilinear motion of the rod on the right produces intermittent circular motion of the wheel by means of the elbow-lever and the pawl. The direction of motion of the wheel is determined by the side on which the pawl works. This contrivance is used in giving the feed-motion to planing-machines and other tools.

23. The piston-rod and crank motion used in the steam-engine. The reciprocating rectilinear motion of the former is converted into the rotary motion of the latter through the agency of the connecting-rod (not shown).

24. An eccentric, such as is used on the crank-shaft of steam-engines for communicating reciprocating rectilinear motion to the slide-valves. It rotates round an axis not pushing through its centre.

25. Internal spring pawls for a ratchet brace. The ratchet can revolve only in one direction (counterclockwise), and as it does so the springs are

gradually compressed and suddenly released in turn.

26. Friction pawl feed motion, silent. The arrow shows the direction of rotation of the wheel. The principle of the contrivance is obvious.

27. A heart-cam, by whose rotation uniform traversing motion is imparted to the vertical bar. The dotted lines show the method of obtaining the curve of the cam. Eight concentric circles are drawn with radii in arithmetical progression as shown, and they are divided into twelve equal sectors. The points on the heart-curve are determined by the intersection of radii and circles.

28. A quick-return crank motion, applicable to shaping-machines. This arrangement needs no explanation.

Mechanical Movements 29. A crank motion, with the crank wrist working in a slotted yoke, thereby dispensing with the oscillating connecting rod.

30. A screw stamping-press, showing how rectilinear motion may be obtained from circular motion by means of a screw.

31. A screw-cutting mechanism. The rotation of the left-hand screw produces a uniform rectilinear movement of a cutter which cuts another screw-thread (seen on the right). The pitch of the screw to be cut may be varied by changing the sizes of the engaged spur-wheels at the bottom of the frame.

32. The movable headstock of a turning lathe. By turning the wheel on the right hand motion is communicated to the screw, thus causing the spindle with the centre at its end to move in a straight line.

33. Swivelling-gear for car wheels. The essential part is the operation of the endless screw on the worm-wheel. The wheels are connected by a lever freely joined to the cranks.

34. Diagrammatic representation of screw-gear to operate three worm-wheels in the same direction, for chucks, etc. The method of working is obvious.

35. A mutilated screw for sliding into a nut having corresponding parts of the thread cut away, to be fixed by a partial turn. It is used for the breech-pieces of cannon.

36. Variable radius lever, operated by a crank motion to give variable

angular reciprocating motion to a shaft.

37. Hand or power feed-gear, for a drill, boring-machine, &c.

38. A method of doubling the length of stroke of a piston-rod or the throw of a crank. A pinion revolving on a spindle attached to the connecting-rod is in gear with the fixed lower rack and also with the upper rack, which is carried by a guide-rod above and is free to move backward and forward. The connecting-rod communicates to the pinion the full length of stroke, and since the lower rack is fixed the pinion rotates, thus making the upper rack travel twice the length of the stroke.

Mechanical Movements   39. A toggle-joint arranged for a punching-machine. The lever at the right operates upon the joint or knuckle of the toggle on the left, thus raising or lowering the punch.

40. A stone-breaker, with chilled-iron jaw-faces and a toggle or knapping motion.

41. An ellipsograph. The oblique traverse-bar carries two studs, which slide in the grooves of the cross-piece. By the motion of the traverse bar the attached pencil is made to describe an ellipse.

42. Link-motion valve-gear of a locomotive engine. The rods of the two eccentrics on the right are jointed to the curved slotted bar called the link, which can be raised or lowered by the system of levers terminating in the handle at the left. The link carries in its slot a slide and pin connected with another arrangement of levers, which operates on the valve-rod as shown. If the link be so arranged that the slide is at its centre, then the movement of the eccentrics will simply cause the link to oscillate about the pin of the slide, and the valve-rod will be at rest. Otherwise the valve-rod will move, and, if the slide be at an end of the link, steam will be admitted during nearly the whole stroke, but if the slide occupy an intermediate position the period of admission of steam is shorter In the latter case the steam is worked more or less expansively.

43. Joy's locomotive valve-gear operated by the connecting-rod. The rod A is connected to the starting-lever to reverse, vary, or stop the distribution of steam by the slide-valve (cf. 42).

44. Side shaft motion for operating Cornish, Corliss, and spindle valves.

Mechanical Movements   45. The "Geneva stop", used in Swiss watches to limit the number of revolutions in winding up. The convex part *a b* of the upper wheel acts as the stop.

46. A form of strap brake used in cranes and other hoisting-machines. If the lever be depressed the ends of the brake-strap are drawn toward each other, and the strap is thus tightened on the brake-wheel.

47. A dynamometer, used to ascertain the amount of useful effect given out by a motive-power. A is a smooth pulley secured on a shaft as near as possible to the motive-power. Two blocks of wood, or one block and a series of straps fastened to a band or chain, are fitted to the pulley, and these are so arranged as to bite or press upon the pulley by means of the screws and nuts on the top of the lever D. At the end of D is a scale, and the stops C, C' prevent the lever from travelling far from the horizontal position. The shaft being in motion, the screws are tightened and weights are placed in the scale until the lever takes the position shown at the required rate of revolution. The useful effect is then represented by the product of the weight added and the velocity at which the point of suspension of the scale would revolve if the lever were attached to the shaft.

48. A diagrammatic sketch of a form of groove for ball-bearings, running horizontally, showing the points of bearing in the grooves.

49. A diagrammatic sketch of a roller bearing for a vertical shaft, with steel balls between the ends of the cone-rollers to separate them and reduce their friction.

50. A diagrammatic sketch of a roller bearing for a wagon axle, with balls between the roller ends to separate them and prevent internal friction. Two views of the bearing are shown in order to make the arrangement perfectly clear.

51. A recoil escapement for clocks. The anchor H L K is made to oscillate on the axis *a* by the swing of the pendulum. The teeth of the escapement-wheel A come alternately against the outer surface of the pallet A and the inner surface of the pallet D. The pallets are not concentric to the axis *a*, and therefore a slight recoil of the wheel takes place after the escape of a tooth (whence the name of the escapement). When the pallets leave a tooth the teeth slide along their surfaces, giving an impulse to the pendulum.

Mechanical Movements   52. A dead-beat or repose escapement for clocks. The lettering is as in the preceding. The pallets are concentric with the axis *a*, and thus while a tooth is against the pallet the wheel is stationary.

53. A lever escapement of a watch. The anchor B is attached to the lever E C, with the notch E. On a disk D, on the axis of the balance-wheel, there is a pin which enters the notch at the middle of each vibration, causing the pallet to enter in and retire from between the teeth of the scape-wheel. The wheel gives an impulse to each pallet alternately as it leaves a tooth, and the lever gives an impulse to the balance-wheel in opposite directions alternately.

54. Chronometer escapement. As the balance rotates in the direction of the arrow, the tooth V presses the spring against the lever, thus pressing aside the lever and removing the detent from the tooth of the wheel. As the balance returns V presses aside and passes the spring without moving the lever, which then rests against the stop E.

55. A parallel motion. To the left-hand end of the short vibrating rod in the centre the radius-rod is connected, to its right-hand end the beam, and to its centre the piston-rod.

56. The working of the pin in the oblique groove of the lower cylinder produces an alternating traverse of the upper shaft with its drum.

57. A drilling-machine. Rotary motion is given to the vertical drill-shaft by the bevel-gearing. The shaft slides through the horizontal bevel-wheel, but is made to turn with it by a feather and groove. It is depressed by means of a treadle connected with the upper lever.

58. Showing how to describe a spiral line on a cylinder. The spur-wheel on the right gears with the toothed rack shown behind, thus causing the pencil to traverse the cylinder vertically. It also produces rotation of the cylinder.

59. Wheel-work in the base of a capstan. The drumhead and the barrel can be rotated independently. If the former, which is fixed to the spindle, be locked to the barrel by a bolt, it turns the barrel with it (single-purchase). Otherwise the wheel-work comes into operation, and the drum-head and barrel rotate in opposite directions with velocities as three to one (triple-purchase).

Mechanical Movements   60. A centrifugal governor for steam-engines. The central spindle is driven from the engine by the bevel-gearing, and the balls fly out under the action of centrifugal force. If the engine speed increases, the balls diverge farther, thus raising the slide at the bottom and so reducing the opening of the regulating-valve connected with it. If the speed of the engine decreases, an opposite result follows.

61. Crank-shaft governor cut-off gear. Two hinged centrifugal weights are coupled by links to the cut-off eccentric sheaves and returned by springs to the full open position.

62. A gas-engine governor. The revolving cam throws the vertical arm of the lever far enough to close the gas-valve when the speed increases beyond the normal.

63. A plan view of the Fourneyron turbine. In the centre are a number of fixed curved "shutes" A, which direct the water against the buckets of the outer wheel B, thus causing it to revolve.

64. The Jonval turbine. The shutes are on the outside of a drum *a*, stationary within the casing *b*. The wheel *c* is similar, with the buckets exceeding the shutes in number and set at a slight tangent instead of radially.

65. Montgolfier's hydraulic ram, by means of which a small fall of water throws a jet to a great height or furnishes a supply at a high level. The action of the water on the two valves, which are alternately open, is easily comprehended. The right-hand one is pressed down by a weight or spring. The elasticity of the air gives uniformity to the efflux.

66. Common lift-pump. During up-stroke lower valve opens and piston-valve closes, and water rushes up to fill the vacuum created. During down-stroke lower valve closes and piston-valve opens, and the water passes through the piston. At next up-stroke it is raised by the piston and passes out by the spout.

67. Common force-pump, with two valves. When piston rises, the suction-valve opens and water enters the vacuum. When piston descends the suction-valve closes and the outlet-valve opens, and the water is forced up through the outlet-pipe.

68. A double-acting piston-pump with four valves.

69. A hydrostatic press. Water forced by the pump through the small pipe into the ram cylinder and under the solid ram forces the latter up. The amount of force exerted on the ram bears to the pressure on the plunger the same ratio as the area of the ram does to the area of the plunger. Thus, if the area of the plunger cross-section be two square inches and that of the ram four square feet, a pressure of ten pounds on the former will produce a pressure of 2880 pounds on the latter, or nearly 26 cwts.

70. The Bourdon aneroid gauge. B is a bent tube closed at the ends and secured at its middle, C. The ends of the tube are connected with a toothed sector gearing with a small pinion which carries the indicating pointer. Pressure of steam or other fluid admitted to the tube tends to straighten it, thus moving the pointer more or less.

71. An air-pump with foot and head valves.

72. Root's rotary engine, used as blower and also as pump. It has two rotating pistons of special shape, so arranged that air or water may be caught and carried forward by their motion.

73. Waygood's patent hydraulic balance lift. A is the lift-cylinder communicating with the interior of the cylinder and ram B. The cylinder C and ram D are loaded to nearly balance the cage and ram A, and the load is raised by admitting pressure water to cylinder C.

74. An epicyclic train. The wheel A, which is concentric with the revolving frame C, gears with F, which is fixed to the same axle as E. E gears with B and D, the latter on the same axis as A. The driving motion may be communicated to the arm and one extreme wheel, A or D, in order to produce an aggregate motion of the other extreme wheel; or motion may be given to the two extreme wheels, thus communicating motion to the arm.

75. Another form of epicyclic train. F G is the arm, secured to the central shaft, A, upon which are loosely fitted the bevel-wheels C, D. The bevel-wheel B turns freely on F G. Motion may be given to the two wheels C, D to produce aggregate motion of the arm, or to the arm and one of these wheels to produce aggregate motion of the other.

76. Common D slide-valve with three ports: a diagrammatic section.

77. Another form of slide-valve, partly in

equilibrium. The arrows show the movement of the steam. (Like the other figures on this plate, this one is a diagrammatic section.)

78. A variable cut-off valve on the back of the main slide, the rod of which (seen above) can be revolved by hand or from the governor to vary the opening of the cut-off valves.

79. Double-beat valve, with sunk seating.

80. Reducing-valve, which can be adjusted by the balance weight to pass fluids from a high to any lower pressure.

81. An equilibrium-valve.

82. India-rubber disc and grating valve.

83. A four-plunger valve, used for double-power hydraulic lift-cylinders employing a trunk piston For the low power the pressure-water acts on both sides of the piston; for the double power it acts only on the back of the piston, the front side being then open to the exhaust.

84. Sketch of the Corliss valve-gear, operated by a single eccentric. It has two steam and two exhaust valves of an oscillating cylindrical type, worked from pins on a rocking wrist-plate. The steam-valves have trips regulated by the governor.

Mechanical Movements   85. Corliss valve, with rectangular rocking spindle.

86. A favourite type of vertical overhead cylinder screw engine, with half-standards and distance rods, one, two, or three cylinders, simple or compound. The condenser is usually in the back standards and the pumps behind.

87. A pedestal bearing, with four brasses and set-screw adjustments.

88. A hydraulic oil-pivot for vertical-spindle. Oil under pressure is forced into the channels between the bearing faces, the area and pressure being adjusted to the load. The surplus oil is returned from the oil-well to the pump.

89. An engine crosshead, with adjustable guide-brasses, set up by taper keys and nuts.

90. An equalizing lever to distribute the load on two car springs.

91. Korting's water-jet condenser. It requires three feet head of condensing water

92. An automatic tipping-scale. When full, to equal the weight, it falls and tips by striking a fixed stop. The scale then turns over and returns to its position to be refilled.

www.ingramcontent.com/pod-product-compliance
Lightning Source LLC
Chambersburg PA
CBHW061205180526
45170CB00002B/975